# The Ramblings of a Dreamer

# The Ramblings of a Dreamer

## Poems
## By Devyn A Baldus

Devyn A Baldus




Cover by 100Covers

Illustrations by Devyn Baldus

# Dedication

*For myself, most of all.*

# Introduction

This book is a collection of all the rambling thoughts that I planned to never share. I was fifteen years old, and I was learning all over again what it meant to love and hurt, to dream and fear. I was philosophizing about the spaces between reality and about the girl in class sitting next to me, all gathered in notebook margin scribblings. The world was too vast and too rigid, and people barely listened without laughing about "young love", "innocence", and "dreamers".

In this world where war and pandemics, eco-disaster and general pandemonium are always sitting around the corner - or hell, just behind our morning coffee - it's easy to worship cynicism. It's easy to believe that the only wise and worthy thoughts are the ones that portray our impending doom and spit in the face of naivety. It's easy to tell each other to "grow up" and really mean, "I'm scared and angry, so you should be too." This is how it's always been. It's the universal cry of humankind: I am afraid.

But it doesn't have to be. I think that's what "growing up" or "wising up" really means. Not living in the fear but learning to put it aside.

When I was young and wrote these words, I feared people would find out about my naive hopes and dreams, so I harbored them behind walls of cynicism and spite. I thought that certainly my feelings were immature and somehow that made them less real. At the time, I would read them back and think, *These don't really make sense, they just ramble on and on about unrealistic feelings.*

I still think that when I read them, but now it's with joy because, *That's what humans are! We're not concise and we rarely make rational decisions! We're a bunch of nerves and feelings coexisting in an uncertain reality and a chaotic society, of course we rarely 'make sense'! But what's vital to realize is that we're individuals shouting unanimously. Humans* are *dreamers - buried deep or loud and proud. We believe we can make things better.*

Around that time that I first started writing, I wrote a letter to my future self, promising to always honor those rambling dreams, even if no one else would. Well, here is my letter back to my younger self: I'm still listening to you. I'm still dreaming. And there's a whole lot of other people listening to you too.

# Disclaimer

Dear Reader,

Some sections of this book address topics that are heavy and difficult to read. I strongly suggest taking breaks between reading to hydrate, rest, and overall practice self-care. It also might be helpful to talk to someone - a friend or counselor - about any feelings and emotions that come up with these topics.

Above all, take care of yourself and know that there's another dawn out there waiting for you.

# Contents

# Prologue

*To read is to dream, guided by someone else's hand.*

-Fernando Pessoa,
*The Book of Disquiet*

One day -
I will print these poems on paper
So they may whisper my words
                    Like ghosts
            Like leaves
Back to the forests of dreamers
And let my messages be carried on tongue
and wind
            Like seeds
To the far reaches of the world

Let my writings be mad and wild
Let them run free -
Let them be like a child let to run
Naked in the sea
And still let there be meaning in their
Beautiful misery
Like the jungles overgrown - untamed
Let patterns lie in their making
Nature's mysteries
Inscribed in each leaf

Who will see my words as I read theirs -
fondly
Who will judge *me* - so tenderly?

# Everything
# I Know
# About
# Daydreams

First I dreamt in the day. I draped reality in a warm cloak, satin and shimmering with hand-spun stars. We create the dreams we see in the day. And I thought, *well, if I could make a dream, wouldn't I spin it pretty and call it love?*

*You fall into daydreams more than you fall
into love
Those mirages sparkle and shine,
Simple though they be –
Eyes to look into your tearing eyes,
Soul to listen to your loud soul -
They radiate in their hopeful beauty
Almost real, taking physical space,
Illuminating the universe –
Or just the dark room -
And sometimes someone steps
Through that mirage
Towards you*

*You must decide
Whether to catch their solid hand
And love their human heart
Or keep falling for a Dream*

Loving is a secret
The kind learned in starlit dreams
And forgotten again
In the harsh light of day

I carry you with me on my emptiest nights
Or rather, on my emptiest nights,
I carry a *You* with me
You don't exist.
But the night is cold
And the stars are cold
And my hands are cold
And so
*You might exist*

I want to experience love
To put a face to the songs I sing,
A memory to the poems I read

*I am just waiting for someone to come and
show me what all the fuss is about*

Oh, the irony of me
Scorning every Romeo
Only to sigh, *I dreamt a boy*
Only to cry, *he didn't show.*

Oh, the agony of me
Biggest hypocrite of them all
Falling in love with a concept
Still, surprised when I fall

Oh God, what did I do -
When I convinced myself - somehow
I'd come back with you:
Your touch, your kiss
The memory of your lips
Your look, your eyes
To hold me through my flight
Your words, your laugh
That I could bring them back
Your voice, your song
Fit inside my carry-on
One glance, all I'd need
To bring you back with me

And now I'm all packed
And now I'm all landed
And bags in my hand
But I'm back empty-handed

25

Your soul haunts me in the most exquisite
and terrible ways

When it comes to love,
We're all nothing more than a set of eyes
Peeking through the blinds
Waiting for someone
To come knock on our door

27

My dreams started whispering of you months
ago, nudging me to make room in my heart

A love like ours, a soul like yours needs lots
of space

I think the ocean is a good place to start

If my imagination
Were a degree less bold,
I'd never know the comfort
Found wrapped in your hold

If my imagination
Were a unit less wild,
I'd never feel the joy
Of catching your smile

If my imagination
Were a touch more dull,
I'd never know of timeless love
That touches the soul


But perhaps these deluded wonders,
If I could not see them
Would also grant me
A touch more freedom

29

If only I loved aloud the way I love in quiet -
I think the world would be a much more
beautiful place.

I long to behold the fields of May
Drink the sunlight in golden sips
But it's March today
And the clouds are gray
So I'll settle for a bouquet of tulips

I fear that I will always be the one
Who's pinning my arms
Behind my back
And swiping my legs from underneath
And pushing my head into the mud
As I desperately try to chase love

I have lived in
four different cities
      three different countries -
         two different continents -
And my favorites were all beside the sea
It seems I return
Whether I mean to or not
It is always calling to me

My heart, my joy, wherever you may be
I believe it must be somewhere
Alongside the sea

Love,
For me,
Will be a fortress
Opening its gates
After a lifelong siege
Blinking up at the bright sun
And learning how to bask in the light.

Dark thoughts raged
*the moment I met you*

They didn't like that, eyes locked on you,
     I could no longer see their
     eerie forms
And ears enchanted by your laugh,
     I could no longer hear their high
     whispers
And tongue whispering secrets to your lips,
     I could no longer taste their bitter
     despair
And nose inhaling your intoxicating cologne,
     I could no longer smell their
     rot
And skin warm from your touch,
     I could no longer feel their frigid
     bite

They knew you for my absolution long
before I ever did

Meeting you was like hearing my favorite
song for the first time -

I didn't know the words
or the notes
or the tune

But my heart danced to your beat
And slowly we found our rhythm

Maybe it's the moon, love
Maybe it's your lips
Or maybe it's the bottle of wine
I've consumed between sips
Maybe it's the doves - or
Their symbolic industry
But if I could reach your hand right now
I'd pull you closer to me

37

Well – love – it happened quite suddenly:

He smiled and I decided I wanted to drink
that happiness straight from his lips.

In the twilight evening's kiss
Under the giggling eyes of the stars
We stagger
Our limbs have folded together
Arm under arm
And leg looped through leg
And head on your shoulder
And without realizing it
*We're falling*
The strings pull tight
And our hearts are knotted.

*I am scared, i don't think i can untangle this
one without anything ripping*

Maybe love is a mirage
And maybe illusions are lies
But all dreamers know
Falsities and truths
Share the same faded line

*confessions:*

1.  I see my hand and feel your thumb
    tracing
circles of starlight across my skin.

2.  My hair brushes against my face and
    the ghost of your hand pushes it back,
coloring me scarlet.

3.  Even turning my head makes my
    neck
    tingle warm
with the memory of your breath's caress.

4.  Everywhere I look,
    i see you,
    and feel you
    and God, you know it.
You flash me that damn smile and know that
I ignite.

I'm addicted to this feeling you give me
Like the whole world is saturated
Like life is suddenly an overripe fruit
And everywhere I look I can see it bursting
with sweetness that wasn't there before

Love, you drive me crazy.
In a storm of you,
I'm a madman clinging to metal,
Begging to be struck.

43

I'd walk with you straight off a cliff if you promised you'd still be next to me at the bottom.

It's strange that at this point I'd give anything
Just to ask how you're doing -
I'd sell my soul
For some small talk

45

And I can never tell if you've woken me from my daydreams or if you're just another one of them.

*your name tastes like cinnamon*

To me,
Your name is a blend
Of warm hope spiced over by ache and
longing
A swirl of memories of lingering touches and
stolen glances,
And I add a dash of dreams of what could be

I sip it and it burns my tongue with a tea-
kettle scream
I blow' on it, a quiet plea for mercy
It doesn't cool -
It never cools -
I sip it again anyways

I am a scientist
But all that I want to study now is her
I am a scientist
And there are stars and galaxies and
supernovas to be observed
But my God - there is also *her*!

Her lipstick must be the night sky draped so
artfully along her mouth
But all the stars have fled to hide behind her
eyes
And when her lips tug upwards to her
cheeks,
like the gentle curve of the Earth
They must think the night is dawning
And they begin to shine

49

Some may have the Sun
And some may have the Moon
And some may have the Stars
But me?
I'll have you

I want to swim in the deepest hollows of your
mind just to hear what echoes there

51

You are the safest arms to ever carry me,
The gentlest soul to ever kiss me,
And the softest heart to ever love me -
I have never felt so treasured and
*It makes me tremble*

My demons have quieted this morning
My angels haven't made a sound
The voices are holding their breaths
And butterflies' wings are bound

All is silent and all is still
In this moment before day dawns anew
Because all others are watching the sun rise
And all of me is watching you

When these words tumble from my mouth,
they fall true
Yet dread coils in my stomach that I will
soon wake anew
For I can feel the first rays of dawn with each
breath I breathe
*You are the first, last, and only dream I will
ever dream*

You are simultaneously
>           Everything I hoped you'd be
And
>           Nothing at all like I expected
And I have come to find that this is -
>           *you are* -
the loveliest of combinations

From golden meadows and
sunny days
My lover did steal me away
To silver waves and moonlit nights
My lover of the Northern lights

If this is a lie,
Lie to me tonight
Lie with me all night
Then sneak out before sunrise
When the truths come back in sight

57

*we can draw our own constellations*

If we are not written in the stars
We'll carve our names as scars
Instead of the heavens -
We'll have our hearts

There's no string tying us together
But I've got some rope and I'm good at tying
knots
And who cares if we're not written in the stars
I'll carve our names into the wooden counter
of this bar
I'll throw down my long, long hair
Or use it to lasso the moon
Then we'll run away together -
The dish and the silver spoon

59

Love, if a lie,
is the lie we choose,
the dreams we write
into daylight

If I could tell you how to love me,
I would ask that you do so unconditionally.
That you stand at my side against a-hundred-
thousand fighting men
That you follow me into the deepest depths
of Hell
That you be my best friend, my partner in
crime
That you make me laugh and listen to me
read and
      throw me into pools and drag me into
      the rain to dance with you
That you never stop trying
That you never stop thinking I'm worth the
effort
That you never think I would ask so much of
you, and yet
That you would be willing to give it all the
same
But I cannot tell you how to love me because
love is not a wishlist to be checked off
Love is a leap of faith, a making and
unmaking
Forged in vulnerability and unguarded trust
That they will do right by you
So, instead, that is how *I* will love *you*,
And, oh, what a gift it is to love you.

My love,
I know sometimes you feel like the entire
world
rests on your shoulders, and I know
sometimes the weight brings you to your
knees and I know you think that you are like
Atlas, and it is your duty to hold up the
heavens but people are not gods and you, my
love...
you are not Atlas.

My love,
When the burden on your back brings you to
your knees, be it on the highest peak of the
tallest mountain or on the cold tile bathroom
floor, I will be there to hold you and pick you
up. And when your knees start to shake and
you fear the heaviness will break you, I will
be there to catch it, to take that weight from
you. My love, people are not gods, so we lean
on each other for help, and you, my love,
you are not Atlas, so you are not meant to
bear these burdens alone.
Lend me a bit of your sky, my love, and let
us carry it side by side, walking through life
until it can learn to stand on its own and we
can together let go.

Her heart did not lie on the surface
I had to dig for it
By the time I reached it,
Meters under the soil
I found I quite liked the earthy caverns
So I planted myself there and grew alongside
her

That is what love is:
Looking for a person's heart and finding a
home there as well.

I may not love you forever,
I can only promise you the now,
But as my heart bears the weight of my love
And its vastness bends the bones of my rib
cage
I must tell you that this feels enough
This *now* holds its own eternity

Again and again,
You pull me back from the brink of my own
darkness
You save me from the extent of my own
misery
You see me sinking, and you pull me back to
the surface
Just by grabbing my hand.

*but sometimes, still, I slip*

The scariest thought I sometimes have
Is that you could've left me long ago
And I would've found myself on that beach
alone,
Wishing on that shooting star -
Not for your happiness,
But just for *you*

Memories are the echoes of the present,
and they sound loudest in dark, empty
spaces,

So I'll try to dance and forget, but when the
music ends,

It'll be your name I'm swaying to.

67

And there's a moment when I wake
That I hold onto the shadows
Behind tightly closed eyelids
That I grasp for the place
Where I can pretend you are with me.

~~Most nights~~
Some nights
I close my eyes and pretend I can still feel
your arms
wrapped around me
Your phantom grasp is all that carries me
into sleep
Anymore

# Everything I Know About Nightmares

I can't always end it by waking up.
Sometimes they follow me.
Sometimes I'm not sure if I'm awake
yet at all, or if what haunts me is just
waiting behind the next corner.
Because nightmares are the things
that happen to us.
And sometimes they don't feel like
terrors. Sometimes they just nestle
like a splinter in your spine instead.
A more subtle haunting.

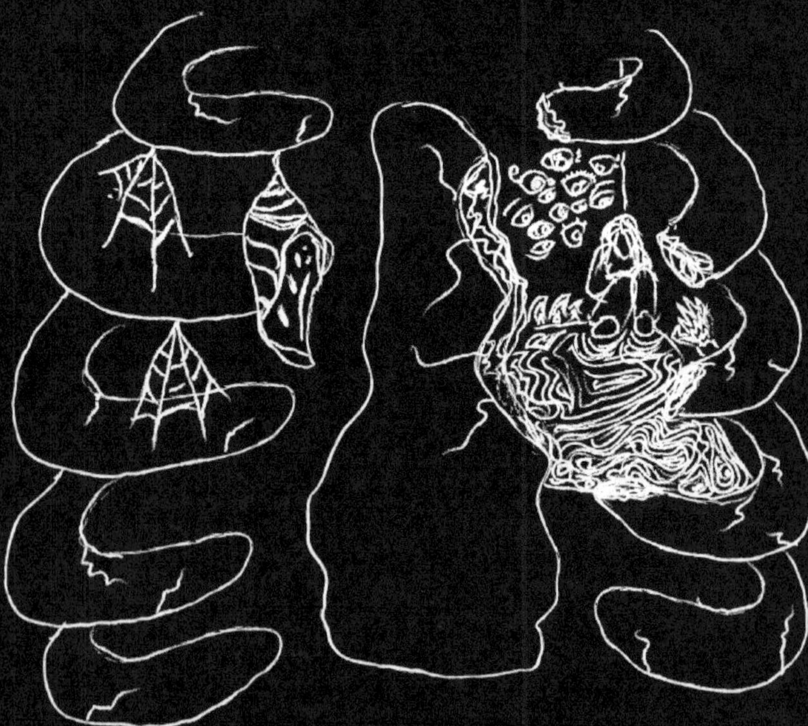

*We're scared*
*We're hurt*
*And we don't know how to make it stop*
*Nightmares are really just these:*

*The cycles we circle endlessly*
*The limbos we live a thousand years*
*Languishing eternally and soundless pleas*
*Or paralyzed in grief*
*And most of all, lonely*

*If we could share our nightmares, they'd*
*cease to be.*

I'm stuck on the way a layer of clear liquid seems
to sit between the glass and the wine - almost
unnoticeable, except to the keen eye
Voices are rising in the background, the air thick
with tension and warring whims
Frustration and pain give way to anger give way to
violence
Give way to noise
         so much noise.
A cacophony of conflict,
but me,
I am stuck on the peculiar level of clear liquid
atop the wine
The glass disappears, along with the wine
A mystery spoiled a moment later by a shattering
song
It's gone under a metamorphosis then - another
victim
Of entropy's relentless pursuit
Teardrops of blood are splattered across the wall,
More evidence of the crime
I lean forward to examine
Not blood-
Wine.

The cacophony reaches a crescendo, the air
hardly breathable,
And I examine the ring of clear
Around the wine droplet on the wall

Again and again - where does it hurt?
I'm not certain - I'm not sure!
But I burn - I burn!

Wild animals live beneath my skin
Whispering to *fight and run*
          *and freeze and fly and hide*
They tear at my insides
and rumble their irritation,
I push them back, hold them down,
Learn to laugh loud enough to drown them
out

But my throat is getting sore, and they are
getting louder

75

he reaches inside me so deep i think he must
be pulling me inside out- and he grips and
twists at my chest so hard, he must be prying
out my heart- and when he smiles over me i
see blood dripping from his teeth and- oh
god get off get off *get off*

Some people can stomach sadness
But me?
I can barely swallow it -
It sits heavily on my tongue

I think I must be
A shape with 47 sharp edges
And I tuck myself in the corner of each room
So I don't prick anyone with the outline of
my many shards
But 47 acute angles don't fit into the 90
degrees between two walls

And I press and I press into that perfect
crease
But my asymmetry always inhibits me
And I file and I cut all of my curves away
But one point becomes two and I gain more
every day

No matter how much I tuck and fold,
*straining*
For that true 90 degrees
I know I can never be a form of perfect
symmetry

My words
   Are
      Running
        Away
          From
            Me
              And
                I
                  Can't
                    K
                    e
                    e
                    p

                    U

                    p

The wind shook the tree
And I watched petals drift down on me
But it was hail that struck my upturned face
And rain that melted down my cheeks

Now I watch storms sheltered
Wrapped warmly in the arms of a sweater
Never leave unarmed with umbrella
Know better than to brave the weather

The night sky doesn't look different
But I think a star has gone out
It feels emptier than before
But maybe it's I who am fading

*the sadness doesn't fight fair*

When it attacks, it clings to your bones and
muscles and turns them to lead until you're
wading through honey to get away.

When it attacks, it comes in the dark where it
can whisper oh so convincingly
>    to *give up,*
>    to *lay down,*
>    to *stop fighting,*
Until you're swinging with your left arm while
your right is pulling you back under the
covers.

When it attacks,
it slides behind your eyes and tells you that
shapes are blurring,
it slips down your throat and tells you that
you're choking on wind,
it coils into your belly and tells you that
your stomach is next to your heart
because you're *falling, falling, falling*
and there's nothing you can do to catch
yourself.

The sadness *never* fights fair.

The flowers sitting in front of me
A bouquet of beautiful variety
From where I'm lying, I can see
They've started wilting - just like me

Let the fog roll in
I'll pull it over my head
And hide from the blaring sun
My skin is sore from old scorch marks
I'm tired of the heat
Tired of the burn
So let the fog roll over
Let it settle inside my head

*when I am to die*

When I am to die,
Let me be asleep
Wandering in worlds
I visit in dreams

When I am to die,
Let it be night
So the stars in the sky
Can be my final sight

When I am to die
Let me not dance
Let me not stumble
Betwixt step and advance

For when I am to die
And die I will
I'd like to believe
The world (*too*) is still

This play-acting is painful when you don't
know your role
It aches to be a bug in a perfect program. A
broken key in a symphony. A missed line in
a playwright.
This is *that* dream - the one where you're
standing center-stage, performing mid-play,
and suddenly realize you don't know the
script.
Except it's not a dream, is it?

I see the panic in her eyes and it scares me
for I know that she would pay in blood, and
skin, and soul
for their nod of approval

Our story began with
*Oh, hello!*

And filled with
Laughter and whispers and banter

And ended with
Silence

And I strain to hear the echo of the never-
voiced,

*Goodbye*

*mirrors and smoke*


If you look inside my mind,
You won't like what you see,
You'll find a girl presented
And she's plain as can be

If you look inside my mind,
Don't get too close
Or you'll find *that* girl
Is only mirrors and smoke

If you look inside my mind,
You might wade through the mist
And find illusions in the glass
That you break with your fist

Don't look inside my mind,
For what you deem the "real me"
You won't find a meek girl
Alone in her misery

In fact,
If you looked inside my mind,
You'd get lost or you'd choke
For there's no girl hiding there
Only mirrors and smoke

I stumble through a field of broken glass
Shards slice into the soles of my feet
And bury deep

When I fall onto hands and knees
The slivers hit bone
And carve their imprint into the marrow

When my shaking limbs collapse my torso
The splinters rupture the ribs' thin cartilage
And puncture heart and lungs

When my neck sinks my heavy crown
The fragments gore thin flesh
And pierce lips and eyelids

And I stagger on,
The carcass of a mirror
*A shattered image*

In my dreams I used to be free
Now even there you haunt me

91

I've left and become a forgotten thing
Or maybe remembered - just unseen
Though what is love, if not being known
And who will see me if I'm on my own

I long for home, but which?
But where, but who?
Where will the longing end
Where can I rest my weary feet

At least here,
I can pretend something waits for me
Something just over the hill
Something just across the sea

93

i'm so tired
i'm so tired of being tired

Hate me -
        But think of me please
Curse my name -
        But speak it please
Spit at my feet -
        But face me please
Scorn me -
        But remember me *please*

Last night, I died in my dream
And I didn't wake

And I think it's because I already know what
it feels like:
That bone-deep desperation to survive
That crippling agony
Then darkness

Slipping out of my body
Trying to claw my way back
Failing.

Hopelessness
Emptiness
Drifting
Watching the dance of life go on
And I am missing my cue

If I died in my sleep
During that dream, last night
I don't know it yet

Pinching myself doesn't work anymore

*it doesn't even feel like a nightmare anymore*

I can't feel the nails biting into my skin

*it doesn't even hurt*

it's all so numb...

*...it's all so dark*

# The Ramblings of a Dreamer

please wake me up

# Everything I Know About Dreams

Dreams can be a way to escape the burdens that hold you down.
They can give you wings to fly above the night terrors.
And sometimes, you just have to run.

*Dreams are truly impossibility*
*Built in the backwards bones of unreality*
*They're past the realm of convention,*
*Harboring the point of invention*
*You can fly only when you know you can fly*
*It will take nothing less than conviction*

These poems are messages in bottles
Cast out to sea
Prayers and wishes that someday,
Someone will remember me

103

*~~I WAS HERE~~*
*I'M* STILL *HERE*

I exist between the space in
*Now* And *Forever*

Incapable of untangling the sensory overload
Of what exists right now

Unable to grasp even wisps of the infinite
expanse
Of what could be

So I process the world through a filter
focusing
Of what might come

I live at the end of the sentence you've just
begun
Idle around the middle of the response I'll
soon relay

This point in reality lies just past my anxiety
of social disgrace
And stops just ahead of my dread over the
gaping pit of uncertainty
This point is my safety
This point is my prison
And every once in a while,
I try to slip through the bars

You rolled into my life like a tropical storm,
You swept me up in your wild form
So sure you were where you were going
I went where the wind was blowing

You flew us so far, across land and sea,
Hand in my hand, along you tugged me
You rolled and swept and spun such force
I held on so long but you blew me off course

And I chased after you,
Who spun the whole world faster and faster
And I called to you,
Who were torn apart, as all natural disasters
And I reached you,
Who left nothing but imprints scattered:
Shards of glass on sidewalks
Palm tree fronds on rooftops
Crumbled plaster on walls

You must have been a hurricane - free by
right of birth
You bent the atmosphere and ripped apart
the earth
You put the world in your mouth, then you
swallowed
And I was simply the breeze that followed

*elastic dreams*

There's a curse in books and stories
They make you dream - beautiful dreams
That don't fit inside reality.
i read
And i stretched
And i pulled like a rubber band -
Imagination lengthening
Hope strengthening
Breathtaking
i stop
And i suffocate,
Too big now for reality
And i struggle, too limp to stand again

I had a dream last night
Of the most incredible things
I had wings on my back
And power in my hands
And the world lay at my feet

My head bore a shining crown
And my voice rang loud and true
And my eyes saw the path to follow
To forge the world anew

When this morning I awoke
I told you, I dreamt incredible things
I told you, I saw the entire world
And of it I wanted for nothing

And you told me you'd dreamt the same
You told me simply, *I dreamt of you*
And I smiled sadly as I lied,
*My love, I dreamt of you too*

I find myself teetering sometimes

on the edge of a cliff, except, here, the drop
is on both sides of me. There is no wind, and
yet, something is pulling at me to decide, to
choose one side or the other, because, I
suppose, that's what life is, all movement and
choices. The feeling is like waking up from a
dream, and on one side you can feel the
warm sheets slipping over your bare feet, yet
on the other, you see the remaining tendrils
of the dream just within reaching distance.
And your insides are in utter tumult arguing
their equally convincing cases on the subject.
To re-attach your mind to your body and
open your eyes, or to dive for the tendrils to
continue weaving the dream you began in
your sleep - to face reality or relinquish to
temptation?

Run
Don't stop
Can't stop
Slow down and the rest catches up
Slow down and it overtakes you
So run
And don't look back
And don't hesitate
And don't slow
And don't think
And don't fear
Just run
Each stride longer
Each step further
Each breath louder
Until your heart bursts
Until your lungs empty
And before you even hit the ground,
Before you feel any pain
Before the rest of the world can catch up,

You're gone.

I belong to the night
To the echoes of foreign howls
To the freedom and savagery
To the silent creatures that prowl

Sometimes I dance
with a snippet of Night
given human form

It shows me its vastness,
a taste of the void
I show it my light,
the brief burn of a storm

These memories we hold
Are stamped in light
But in the space between waking
I recall one born of night
A glimpse of something half-remembered-
Observed without senses
In *this* world made senseless
Too strange for our few dimensions
Rippling down a cord's tension
*I strum- strain to hear what strange music it sung*
*Note hangs mid-suspension*

113

Oh noteless song
Oh back-spun dream
Let me sing notes backwards
Let me peek through the seams

In the frigid night, I awaken
Under the black sky where the stars burn
cold
The winds' greedy tongues lick the heat from
my skin,
they steal the fire in my heart and
I'm *moondrunk*

This coldness aches -
But I prefer it
To its more nauseating cousin:
The stifling heat
Of a stranger's arms around me
And still feeling lonely

There are oceans in her body
I hear waves crashing in her breath
And sometimes her hands are so cold,
Eyes so dark, that I know
She carries creatures that don't need light to
survive

There are oceans in her body
And I'm standing at her shore
*Your cold doesn't scare me*, I whisper
Submerging unflinchingly in her icy depths
And when drops of ocean roll down her
sand-spotted cheeks
I lick the warmth away

I want to consume knowledge and
experiences, I want to read all night by
candlelight and stitch my own clothes with
thread that I dye, grow the food that I cook
myself. I want to drive into the sunrise and
sleep in my car and explore towns where no
outsiders can pronounce the name correctly.
I want to be a vessel of literature and culture
and beauty, but with each tidal wave of this
hunger, I know that an emptiness pools
behind it, waiting to pull me into oblivion.
And how can I devour life before I again lose
my appetite?

I forgot what it felt like to be proud of myself
And more than anything,
I miss the sound
of my own voice cheering me on

In the darkest hour
I remind myself that the clock keeps ticking
I take solace in the fact that even I
Cannot *fuck up* so badly
That the 12 doesn't eventually return to 1
And the night doesn't eventually give way to
day

In the darkest hour
I remind myself
That when our eyes betray no secrets
Our ears tell the greatest truths
And I strain to listen for the whispered
*tick tock tick tock tick tock*
Within the steady beatings of my heart
That tell me the world still moves
And soon, light will strike anew

I wonder how many times I've fallen because
I thought it came after the jump.

And I wonder what would happen if I chose
not to fall,
no matter how much pressure
pushed me down, told me to crumble-

I wonder if I could fly?
I wonder if I could fly.

Dreams *and dandelion puffs* are fragile things
People like to stomp, snuff out their
possibilities
But dreams *like dandelion puffs* are also
seeds
They plant ideas not so easily
Extinguished by fear and insecurity -
Ideas cannot be restricted entirely
Even when they end, *new* dreams spring free

There are dreamers on the streets
Hands upturned, down-turned eyes
They're praying, but not to us -
to the gods above,
The younger gods who from the skies,
carelessly signed
the fates of the streets

There are dreamers above the streets
Hands full, empty eyes
their prayers are silent now, more idle
thought than hope -
gods don't pray

There are dreamers below the streets
Hands open, closed eyes
They hold the streets, hold the towers, hold
the skies
Their fate is that of Atlas
They dream of letting go, letting the towers
sink, but bricks don't choose what burdens
they lift
do the dead still pray?

There are dreamers in the streets
Hands lowering, lifting eyes

They're pretending the coins they drop are
enough, pretending chance didn't give them
shoes, pretending the gods in glass towers
aren't their gods too
They're praying for more coins to drop,
praying for better shoes to keep, praying that
the other dreamers will stop one day on the
streets and tear down the beams supporting
the imposters calling themselves Supremes so
the glass can dissolve, and the coins can fall,
and they can all get off the damn streets.

*take me where the rain falls up*

I dream of a world where the rain falls up
The splattered bits pull shakily off the ground
and reach for one another
They fly as one, turning cold and shaped
until colliding once more in the clouds
I dream of a world where flying means rising,
not falling

Dreams are swift rivers
They scare those who cannot swim
But the dreamers cannot drown
So they jump - *they jump in!*

Devyn A Baldus

The words

    tumble

                          paper

                    my

           over

                                        l

                                        i

                                        k

                                        e

                        spilled

                   Ink

        And

              I

                      am

                           a

        Powerful Pen,

           *guiding the chaos*

That is the story of dreamers - of butterflies:
In the dark they unbecome - we all do
Alone, they transform - we all do
Then light breaks through - and this is where
The dreamers diverge
They find the bravery to leap into it
They find they have wings now

Life happens *to* us,
Just like nightmares, you see
Only in dreams can we shape our reality
So I hold them tight when I wake -
I bring them with me

# Everything I Know About Awakening

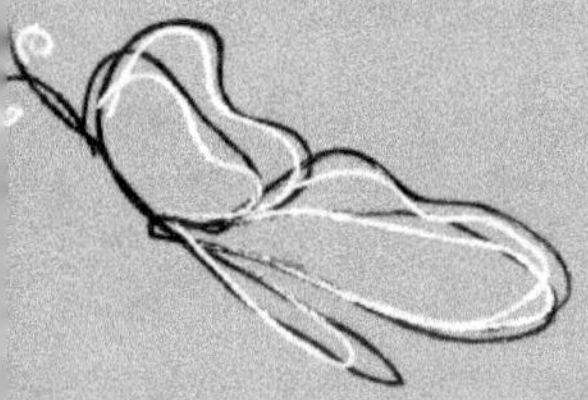 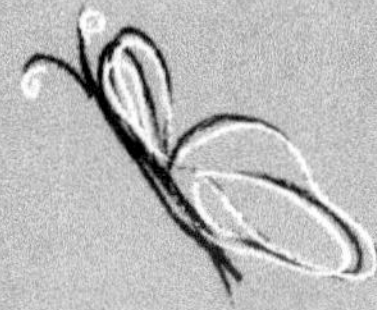

When you wake, bring your dreams with you.
Clutch them tightly in your fists
They carry messages for you,
Secrets whispered by the stars
Too easily we forget them in the day
So hold your dreams closely, when you awake.

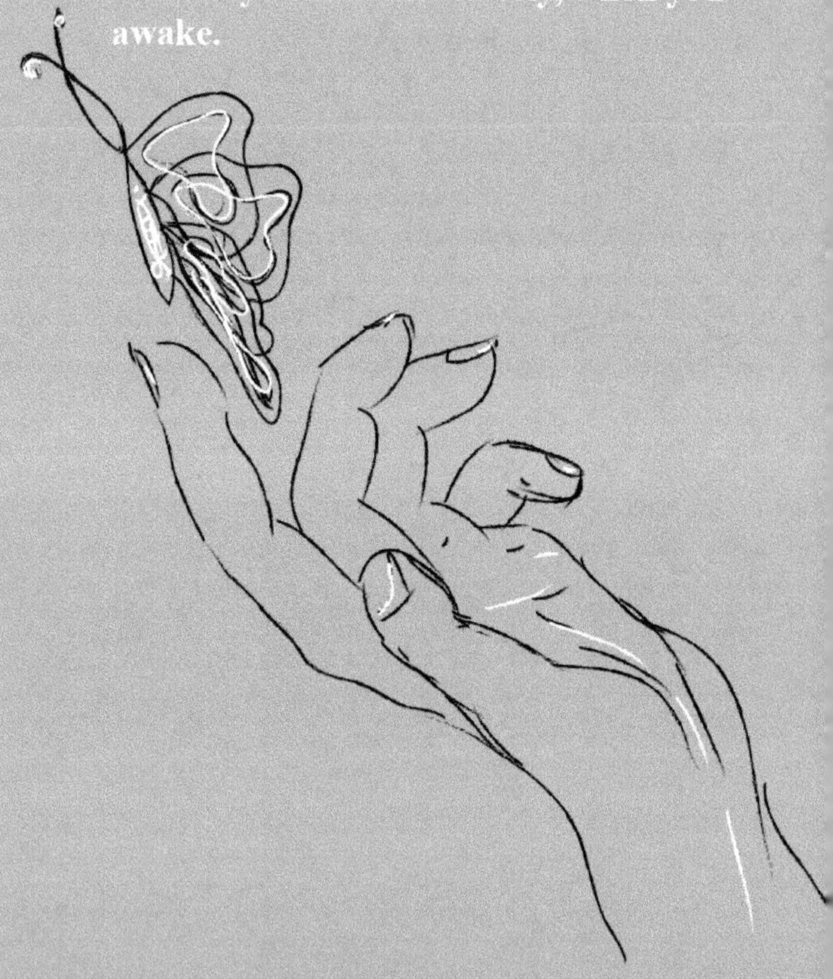

131

*When you're ready to relent your lonely
retreat
When you're ready to surrender your
cynicism and spite
When you're ready to yield the comforts of
your fear
When you're ready to wake:
    Wake
    Dream and still wake
    Wake, truly wake,
    and wake flying*

Sometimes there is strength in fighting,
drawing a line in the sand
saying, *no, you go no further*

133

Sometimes there is strength in flying,
knowing the staying only leaves you trapped
saying, *no, you hurt me no longer*

These words are pain and sorrow,
elation and hope,
truth and lies,
but most of all -
They are an unburdening of a heavy mind

135

These arms that swing
These arms that lift
These arms that sway and shrug and shift

These arms that learned finally
They were also made for holding me

It's a bad habit to scratch at old wounds
And I think it's time to let them heal

They will try to constrain you, child -
they fear the changes you will bring.
Everything you touch turns magic
Take your path, child
And your footprints will glow a path out of
the cave
Let them choose whether to follow it
But do not let their hands pull you down
Nor cover your eyes,
Nor muffle your voice

If your eyes have been opened, never let them be shut again.

Such joys,
Simple joys

I've found in my alone
A beautiful cafe with extra large scones
A kind face on a quiet, stone street
A cathedral's bench and a brand new read

I forgot these things
Spent such time starving


'Til I remembered the light
Of such simple delights

Oh,
What a window and tea
And a stormy sea
Can do,
Can heal for me

The way you see me...
You show it to me so simply, offhandedly
Like pulling a Polaroid out of your pocket
Like you've had it all along
Like it's obvious
But I've never seen me like this
I ask if I can hold onto it -
Just for a little while -
And I hold it so preciously,
Blushing and tears-welling each time
I see how I look through your eyes

It took me a while to see that there are stars
in my eyes
And it took me even longer to see that *I* am
the one who puts them there

The wind ushers the clouds hobbling through
the sky
Here the wind holds still, points to ground to
show
Names each human constellation, and many
does it know
The clouds murmur and cheer, piling
together to peer
In their excitement begin to snow, on the
people down below
The wind rounds them now, pushing the
blundering melee
To guide them onward again, across open
sea

I want to fall in love with the clouds
Again and again, each morning that I wake

145

He told me that the world will be what we make it - for we hold the quill and the paper is blank. So, I will write of a world where love is true and people are good and despair is not ash settling over all things good but a wisp of smoke blown away in the wind. And I will write it and believe it and whisper it like a prayer under a starless night until it becomes my reality.

Let us not waste another moment
Because life will not come running to us
It is a gift that has already been given
It is a gift that we must accept

With our eyes, with our words, with our
hands,
*Let's take it back*

And the smallest of stars stopped to keep us
warm
And the coldest of rocks reflected light
for the dark of our nights

The small ones never forget to look out for
those smaller
The cold ones never forget to extend a warm
cloak

The Universe is a small act of kindness -
one after the next, after the next
Keep paying it forward,
And Life and Love may never end

I look at this expanse - this breathtaking view
Oceans and cliffs and ancient builds
And this feeling in my chest -
This wonder - tastes an awful lot
Like despair
And I'm laughing and grinning and I think
I'm also crying

Daughter, the rain is a gift too.

*Everything.*
What do you want?
Everything. Everything. Everything.
What do you want?
Mouth wide open in the storm
To catch the wind and rain and lightning
bolts
Everything. Everything. Everything.
What do you want?

Laugh with the tears
Smile through the fears
Dance in the rain
Then do it all again

Oh, what lies I was told -
That they would shun me,
A dreamer in *The Real World*
A pink-yellow-blue kind of hue in the bleak

Oh, what lies we were told -
That we are the oddity.
In my travels I have found
More alike than unlike me

Oh, what lies you told -
How did we ever believe?
When the future we dream
Is already here, beginning

I knew the first time that I met you
The two of us could rattle the stars
Cause we're walking the same paths
As everyone else
But our hands are outstretched,
Reaching for Mars

We're the Dreamers
With heads stuck in the clouds
We're the heroes that they prophesied
I know how this story
Always seems to end
But, not us, my love,
We're staying alive

I'm suspended in the inhale before great moments. I'm stuck in the oxygen sucked in before blowing out the candles. I'm stuck in the breath I breathe in before whispering that 11:11 wish with eyes closed and fingers crossed. I'm stuck pulling in that lungful of air before yelling my victory to the world as I stand at the peak of the mountain I've just climbed, staring at the world laid bare before me. I'm stuck in that breath of maybe's and possibly's and it just might be's. I'm stuck in that breath I steal the moment before falling, the second before gravity takes hold of me, the breath before my body hits the water and submerges. I'm suspended here with lungs full and body tense, ready to wish, to yell, to fall, all a mess of uncertainty but shining with this glowing sun of hope. Because I'm falling into this beautiful possibility of something good, armed only with the breath I grab in that split second before, and I know for the first time in my life... that will be enough.

And the biggest fear I know
Is to stare at my paper and have nothing to
write
And my biggest fear, I know,
Is to have all of this pain and sorrow and
elation in my chest
And nowhere to put it down

What if the words don't come
But the pain stays
What if the pen doesn't write
For years and months and days
What if I'm nothing, I'm worthless
What if I'm all the things they say
What if the words that do come,
Are like me - unworthy of the space

But what if I write *one* thing
To which someone else can relate
What if I can help just one person
With the art that I create
What if I can overcome
The fear of that blank template
What if I can be great?
What if I can be great.
What if I can be great!

Then I initiate.

The Ramblings of a Dreamer

# Acknowledgements

There are more names than I could ever list that have led to the creation of this book. I will still do my best to thank them all.

To all of my friends and family - the ones who've been with me since the beginning and the newer faces - I am so lucky to have you in my life. You give me strength and you bring me joy. Without you I would've never learned to dream.

To Mom - you've been my number one supporter. You've read *every* version of my manuscript with unfailing patience and faith in me. You continuously reminded me throughout the past two years to take my time writing this book. You've been proud of me every step of the way, and you've made me feel nothing less than miraculous. Thank you.

To Taryn - you know me better than anyone else in the world. I know I wouldn't even have to write anything here, and you'd still know what I'm meaning to tell you (probably a side effect of you being the primary listener to my rants, my involuntary book buddy, and my main voice of reason). The first copy of this book is all yours. To the dreamers, eh?

To Dad - I know I get my fantastic rhymes from you... but mostly I want to thank you for teaching me to look at the situations logically. This book needed more than feeling to be created.

# The Ramblings of a Dreamer

To Papa - you collected all of the poems I wrote as a child. You were the first to teach me that my words had worth, and it's a lesson that's led me here today. Thank you for being my foundation.

To Nana - you taught me compassion, generosity, and (arguably) a few swear words. Thank you for being such a bright light in my life.

To Alec – for pushing me and looking out for me.

To AunDee - you waited until I was ready, and then you showed me that the support I have spans lifetimes.

To Leslie - for showing me a certain kind of strength called "ground-breaking".

To Dennis and Pennis – for all the support, the trips to Goodwill, and the company on my slow descent to madness.

To the Galway girls – for teaching me how to grab my freedom and for your unquestioning friendship (and for all the great quotes).

To the spider that lived behind the sink in my bathroom throughout my months in Galway - thank you for not leaving your space behind the sink... also, for killing that other spider that tried to move in.

To Eve - you bought me a little blue book, once upon a time, when I was trying to find meaning in my life. Thank you for reminding me what I am capable of. (Also sorry for putting you after the spider.)

To all the strangers who've offered me smiles or kind words, to my various Spotify playlists, to poets and artists, to dreamers... Thank you for inspiring me.

And finally, to the dreamers - the world is yours.

Stay Tuned for Book 2 in the
*Ramblings* series:

# *The Rantings of a Radical*

# The Ramblings of a Dreamer

**Devyn A Baldus** is a first-time self-published author, a world traveler, and an engineer. She's a lover of stories, people, and the stars. Through her writing, she aims to be an advocate for young voices and for the LGBTQ+ community.

*The Ramblings of a Dreamer* is her first published work, and only the beginning of a long writing career to come.

www.devynabaldus.com

@devynabaldus
@devynabaldus

The Ramblings of a Dreamer

www.ingramcontent.com/pod-product-compliance
Lightning Source LLC
Chambersburg PA
CBHW070901160726
48004CB00003B/1187